ODE, C.T.

rley and Mark   ghton

THE YORK, BEVERLEY AND MARKET WEIGHTON RAILWAY

by C.T. Goode.

Front Cover: An Edwardian directors' outing at Kiplingcotes, where there was an abundance of station lamps and neat borders.. Possibly the air was therapeutic as well. The engine, with the number rather badly stencilled on the buffer beam, was rebuilt X2 2-2-4T No. 1679, attached to a carriage for push -and -pull use.
Copyright: Keeper, The National Railway Museum, York.
Ref. No. NRM/1198/79.

Back Cover: A Timetable from the 1850s

© 2002

No part of this book may be reproduced, stored in a retrieval system, or transmitted in any form, or by means electronic, mechanical, photocopying, recording or otherwise without the prior permission of the Publishers and the Copyright holders.

ISBN 1 870313 23 2
72 Woodland Drive Anlaby, Hull HU10 7HX

Printed by: Burstwick Print & Publicity Services,
Burstwick Services Ltd
13a Anlaby Road, Hull. HU1 2PJ

YE 385

9 00 5865997

Contents

Foreword

Still the lines keep coming along to record; this one is of particular interest as it formed part of a major route between Hull and the north of the country. At present, however, I feel that the supply of new material is almost exhausted, unless someone comes up with a bright suggestion. Among primary sources of knowledge such as Messrs. C.J. Allen and K. Hoole, others have been Mr. D. Sillince who wrote two articles found in the 'Railway Magazine for Nov. and Dec. 1965, and a well written work by Mr. Stephen Chapman entitled 'Hudson's Way'. Shots of moving traffic have, however, proved difficult to come by, except at Market Weighton and Beverley, where the photographer had more trains to bring him to those places than stopped at, say Cherry Burton or Fangfoss. Not many of us had easy car riding in those days!

Thanks, too, to those beavering library staff at Beverley and Hull Local Studies Depts. and the York Library. I have always kidded myself that it was a change for them to go in search of old Ordnance survey maps rather than family histories! A special word, too, for the help given by the K. Hoole Centre at Darlington North Road station.

C. TONY GOODE
Anlaby, May 2002.

EAST RIDING OF YORKSHIRE COUNCIL	
9005865997	
Browns Books	25/03/04
385.094 283	8.25
BER-LOCL	

Trevor House

1 Settlements and Beginnings.

In considering the line which ran south eastwards from the vigour of the route from York to Scarborough, one cannot help, certainly in the early years, taking along with it a similar route from the NER main line at Selby. Both ran through flat and quite neat, though often featureless scenery, both had a river crossing on the way, and both ended up initially at Market Weighton, a small, self-contained market town of some 4,700 inhabitants today, with much history about it. The two lines ran into what was at first a terminus, for though an idea had been mooted that the line from York would cross the hills to reach the Hull-Bridlington route at Beverley, as yet nobody had been ready to float the necessary capital. In the case of the Selby line travellers had to wait another fifty years before the hills, much more daunting, were breached towards Driffield.

The reader may not care overmuch for historical background, and it is perhaps more convenient to dispose of it first of all, rather than encountering large chunks later on. On the York to Beverley run there were three towns or villages of particular interest, Market Weighton, Pocklington and Stamford Bridge. The first is the most rewarding in detail.

The first known settlement was on the hill to the east of Market Weighton, at Arras around 400 BC, when the Parisii brought iron age culture from France. Here, in the 19th century a large burial gound was excavated with graves for 500, of whom 50 were women complete with beads and other finery, including also a warrior queen with chariot and horses. Here also was a king buried in full splendour. The Romans reached Britain in 43 AD and set about attempting to quell the Brigantes who lived north of the Humber. In this they had some success after fording the estuary at Brough and setting up headquarters at Malton and York, the former being the major settlement. The Romans came from the river north along the road to South Newbald, where the way divided, the left fork heading for York via Thorpe-le-Street, the other passing mainly through fields to Malton; both kept clear of Market Weighton, though it is said that there was a camp at Delgovicia in the township or at Shipton or Londesborough. Many coins have been found in the area.

St. Helen's Well was set up by the Romans on the way to Malton, firstly for refreshment and next for holy purposes. To this day the well still runs into a concrete basin. After c. 410 AD the emperor Constantine III began to withdraw his legions as, gradually the locals and invaders began to settle their differences and live in harmony.

The name 'Wegtun' was given to the local camp site, the 'town on the road'. Another name was 'Vetun' 'holy town', so called by Edwin, the christian king of Northumbria which included Yorkshire at the time, who owned a summer palace at Londesborough where he received St. Paulinius in 627. Together with his high priest Coifi he was persuaded to ride to Goodmanham, where they threw down the idols and sacked the temple, replacing it by a christian church of wood. Here Coifi was baptised, Edwin, likewise in the new wooden cathedral at York in the same year.

Market Weighton station from the west. A pre-1939 view with overall roof.   *Copyright: D.Thompson.*

Railway bridge at Stamford Bridge. Possibly an early view.
Copyright: K. Hoole Collection.

Next came the Danes, a rough lot who, however, managed to settle down with the Saxons before the Normans came under William, who provided some ruthless, though systematic and industrious parcelling out of land. Thus we now arrive at the 'Wicotun Hundret' of the Domesday Book. The manor of Market Weighton was taken on by various names, including the de Bromefletes, the Vencis and the Cliffords of c.1570, the latter incumbent being in charge of the fleet against the Spanish Armada. At this period the Lord of the Manor lived on Londesborough Rd. near the site of the future railway station.

Up to the 14th century there were no less than 16 ways of spelling 'Weighton', printing coming along before very long to regularise matters to some extent. I am certain that the reader would like to try a hand at attempting to write down all 16 if possible, and a complete list appears at the end of the book.

In 1251 a charter was given by Henry III to Reginald Fitzpeter for a Thursday market, this granted again to Sir Henry de Bromflete by Henry VI in July 1458 for Wednesdays only. In 1703 the Manor descended to the 1st. Earl of Burlington who was now the resident at Londesborough Park.

An early view of Market Weighton station, taken from the church roof. Notice the farmer's barn in the foreground.

Copyright: Beverley Libraries.

The most famous local inhabitant of Market Weighton was William Bradley, a giant born on 10th February 1787, the fourth son of a family of twelve, his father being a butcher. Everyone else appears to have been normal, but William weighed 11st. at 11 years of age and, when fully grown reached 7ft. 9in. and weighed 27st. As would be most likely in these days he was taken on by a local showman and toured as a 'freak', actually reaching George III at Windsor who presented him wth a watch and chain. After ten years or so he returned home in poor health to a house built for him on Market Hill, where he died at the age of 33 years.

Hints of the Industrial Revolution were on the horizon in 1772 when work began on a local canal which was to run from Faxfleet on the Humber to a point some two miles south of the town. Benefits soon showed in the use of bricks and tiles in new houses, brought up from factories on the river bank. However, expectations that the canal would assist in draining the land were not realised and after a long and gracious decline the waterway closed in 1917.

In 1846 the Manor of Weighton and the Londesborough Estates were purchased from the 6th Duke of Devonshire by one George Hudson MP, Lord Mayor and Member for York. Mrs Hudson, a perfectly normal lady, was once heard to say that she could not keep pace with her husband's elevations, as she put it. In due time two of the lines to Market Weighton opened and Hudson was able to halt trains between York and Market Weighton from a platform by the lodge at the end of a long, tree-lined drive. This ostentation or privilege lasted for four years, as in 1850 his financial juggles came a cropper; he had to forfeit the Manor and Estates among other items, the house being sold to the Hon. Albert Denison Conyngham. The latter's coat of arms became the Londesborough crest. King Edward VII was ever a visitor of country seats and, after Denison took charge in 1900 stayed at Londesborough in the following year, the year of his accession. Travel was by rail to Market Weighton. Winston Churchill was entertained at Londesborough Hall during the two weeks of his honeymoon in the area

Market Weighton does not seem to have had festivities for any of the four railways which reached the town over the years; possibly their impact was too small in a busy little place, though they must have noticed the importance of the level crossing which would stop activities from time to time. In Pocklington access was interrupted on two routes in and out of town.

Pocklington must have been a sleepier place than Market Weighton, with no   turbulent earlier history and a lack of direct through traffic. The grammar school was founded in 1514 and was vastly rebuilt in the 19th century when it became the responsibility of its own governors rather than endowed by St. John's College, Cambridge. In 1944 the school became direct grant and independent in 1976 with some 675 boys and 90 mixed juniors, plus some girls in 1991.

The canal mentioned above arrived later than did that at Market Weighton, with the Act approved on 28th May 1815. Its course ran from the Derwent at East Cottingwith to a point on the Hull-York road. The bed was dug out to a depth of nine feet, with three overbridges and nine locks. The engineer was George Leather who had created Goole Docks; he completed the canal for less than the estimate of £43,000.8s. which was remarkable, even in those days. Inwards would come coal, lime and manure, while out would flow corn and flour. From 1834 passengers would be conveyed to Leeds and Wakefield every 3-4 days, while Hull drew the short straw with a service only every 10 days. Thus matters proceeded until 1848, when the York & North Midland bought out the canal company for £18,000 and allowed things to decay. In 1932 the 'Ebenezer' worked along the canal for the last time.

Pocklington was, like many other places, affected by the Railway Mania of 1845, when a project of George Leeman of York was aired under the name of the York & Hull, East & West Yorks. Railway, which meant in plain terms a line from York to Market Weighton with a branch from Pocklington to Driffield which would encounter very stiff terrain. Leeman asked his solicitors to make every effort to gain support from the influential gentry of the neighbourhood, these including George Legard of Fangfoss Hall, Sir Charles Anderson of Burnby and Mr. Read of Hayton. Robert Denison of Londesborough was uncommitted, while Lady Muncaster of Warter was against. A similar line proposed by George Hudson enjoyed the favour of Baron Hotham, Lord Stourton, Sir Edward Vavasour of Holme (who had built his own private canal) and William Constable Maxwell of Everingham. Hudson did not favour the Pocklington-Driffield offshoot and made certain of winning the contest by purchasing the vast

Londesborough Estate over which the line would run. Thus this property would become a pawn in a seedy financial game. In 1846 Hudson obtained an Act for an East Riding Branch of the Y & NM to be built to Market Weighton from York. Stations were to be designed by G. T. Andrews, and the fine building at Pocklington with its all-over roof now preserved as the school's gymnasium appeared in the list of the country's top Victorian stations in 1981.

At the outset the Rev. Thos. Shield, master of the grammar school, objected that the nearness of the station would endanger his pupils - surely not due to the amount of traffic which materialised! There was an increase in illegitimacy due to the extra curricular activity of navvies; there was a large tannery and a growth in weaving, wool spinning, glove making, a ropery and milling. However, by 1851 only the milling, malting and ropery were left as of any importance, workers now being able to travel away to seek work and products more readily brought in. One defunct industry was the culling of the hordes of rabbits to be found on the lower slopes of the Wolds.

Again there was no evidence of public rejoicing when the trains began to run; the railway employed locally eight men and there was one boatman.

To mention Stamford Bridge is to turn back the historical clock once more. The 'bridge' of the title no longer exists, though there are two, the brick rail viaduct and a narrow road replacement of 1727 which has recently borne the brunt of severe flooding by the Derwent. Here was the last victory of the Saxons when, in 1066 Harold met his brother Tostig and Hardrada, king of Norway who had sailed up the Humber with 60,00 men in 300 ships - this alone would have been a wonderful sight for the eyes and ears. On a day in September the battle was fought without ceasing. Harold won a great victory, but he himself had to hurry to the south coast where, near Hastings he joined battle with William the Conqueror and was slain. A fine mural drawn by local children currently adorns the outside wall of the public conveniences by the road bridge.

2. The East Riding branches

From the beginning the Y & NMR had secured an Act of 18th June 1846 for a line to run from the York & Scarborough line to the Hull & Bridlington line via Market Weighton. On the same day an Act was also granted for a line from Selby to Market Weighton, both under the East Riding Branches Act of 1846, with which was a line from Leconfield (Arram) to Hornsea which seems to have sunk without trace, though it was marked clearly on the early tile maps which appeared at all the major stations on the NER system. Even as far back as 1845, what might be called 'the Hull faction' was very active, protective of its trade and anxious to promote its own route, as did actually happen with the opening of the Hull & Barnsley line in 1885. What was envisaged at first was a line leaving the Hull & Selby route near Brough which would run north for ten miles or so through the Caves and Newbald to Market Weighton where the York line would be joined. This would be a sensible idea over flat terrain, and one whch was first aired when the H & S was being built, when George Hudson promised that it would be added. The line carried the sonorous title of the Hull & Great North of England Railway Co. However, Hudson was to leave the scene in a hurry, the turmoil of the bursting of the Mania bubble forced the promotors to pull out, leaving the two solicitors involved to pay what was owing to creditors out of their own pockets. In March 1948 a meeting under Mr. Egginton stressed the value of such a line and requested that the Y & NM be asked to construct the same.

Not everyone was so anxious for this to happen. The vicar of South Cave wrote in a letter that he would be unable to feel favourable to the idea on moral grounds. He wrote that the scum of Hull would make it another place for their Sunday revels and that in his view "the country youths go to a neighbouring town for a 'lark' and the rag-tag-and-bob-tail of towns come into the country, not for sober enjoyment but for Sunday dissipation". So much for that.

The 'peculiarly constructed bridge' at Kiplingcotes. Actually this is not unusual in brickwork for a skew crossing. Copyright: C.T. Goode.

In 1856 a further attempt was made to float the Hull & Market Weighton Railway, with Hudson and the turbulent vicar now out of harm's way, backed now by 17 landed and qualified sponsors and the Mayor of Hull, Alderman Bannister, all with a brief 'to connect the fertile and populous neighbourhood through which the line will pass with the Port of Hull and the markets of the Manufacturing Districts'. It was pointed out that, quite rightly the course of the line would be easy and level, without need for cuttings or embankments. With the adoption of only a single line the route had to be profitable. The NER however, in spite of much support for the line proved obdurate and favoured the more scenic route to Beverley, forcing the solicitors once more to have to pay costs themselves. The thinking no doubt went that, if such a north-south line were built any benefits would be eroded by an east-west line which might come into being in the future - a strong portent of the arrival of the Hull & Barnsley line in 1885.

On the York-Market Weighton line the firm of Jackson & Bean began working to a contract of £116,009 in November 1846 and from Selby in January 1847 at a cost of £81,598. In both cases progress was swift and uneventful, with one river crossing on each. The stations on both lines were built by Burton & Son to the design of G. T. Andrews as found elsewhere on the NER system. One distinctive feature of design was to have pairs of chimneys on the bungalow gatehouses mounted on brick saddles with daylight showing through. The York-Market Weighton line was completed four days later than scheduled, on 4th October 1847. The Selby line would have been completed two months later, but was delayed until 1st August 1848 by another of those plaguey vicars, this time the incumbent at Bubwith who jibbed at the location of the station in his parish, most likely because it was too near the church and not, as he put it, in the 'high field'. At least his choice would have been nearer the main road than what actually resulted. The NER was to build a station at "High Field' a little later on.

Additionally the goods platforms had to be built a little lower where they occurred than those on the York line, to cause more minor bother.

George Hudson was up to his financial trickery, in a manner which has been often found in the past and will, alas often continue in the future. His first move was to secure big profits from his sales of lands acquired at Huntington, Londesborough, Shipton and Market Weighton over which the railway would pass, then quickly claiming compensation for the loss of revenue of lands lost, not a very cunning move really as he was soon spotted, leading to tense and angry scenes in the Bankruptcy court which led, eventually, to Hudson's end as a prominent figure.

A good overall view of Earswick station, looking east from the signal box, with the factory premises in the background.

Copyright: P. Wilson.

In 1851 there were eleven permanent way men and three in the coaching dept. working along the Selby line. At Holme an extra porter was set on for the potato season. The line was described as 'delightful but with next to no passengers to travel'. At Huntington in August 1851 the income barely covered the station master's wages, so it was resolved to close the site and leave the station house for the platelayers. Eventually someone relented and Mr Naylor, who had feared for his post was allowed to live rent free on the premises as long as he worked the crossing gates.

Getting across from Market Weighton to Beverley was no easy matter, physically as well as financially. Hudson's performance had put off the more nervous sponsors of the scheme and among many others, and Lord Dalton of Dalton Holme laid down restrictions for any line likely to cross his property and was undecided as to whether he would benefit more from a halt at Goodmanham than anywhere else. In fact he secured both Dalton Holme and Enthorpe stations, neither of which was of any use to the general public. Shareholders met in 1849 to affirm that, without an extension of some sort the whole scheme was useless; trains from Market Weighton to Hull were travelling miles off a direct route by a zig-zag path through Selby. In the following year the Beverley faction held a meeting to ascertain what was afoot, and the lapse in time now meant that the time span for the Act had run its course, making it null and void. As recorded above the Hull faction pressed on with their proposal for a line from that town to Market Weighton via Brough, opposing the NER. Eventually, however, in 1860 the NER came round once more to the Beverley proposal and a fresh Act was obtained on 30th June 1862. Work began in September, though there was still disagreement with Lord Hotham as to the location of his station - perhaps a mobile one would have sufficed? The new line appears to have been single for many years, as was the sister route from Selby. Stations on the latter were, as well as the two originals at Holme and Bubwith located at Cliff Common, Duffield, Menthorpe, Foggathorpe and Harswell, all suffixed 'Gate', denoting a halt either some way off from the place served, or with rudimentary platforms. The GWR went in for the term 'Road' instead. Duffield Gate did not last long, while Menthorpe Gate kept its

Warthill station looking west . The Sand Hutton yard was in the yard on the right. *Copyright: K. Hoole Collection.*

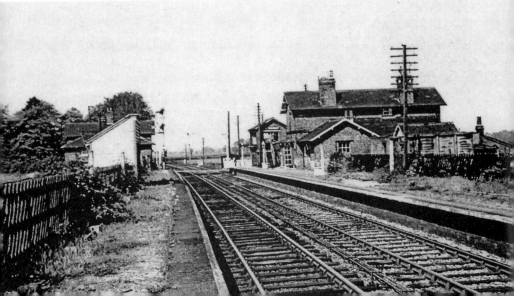

suffix when the others lost theirs. Harswell Gate became Everingham after the village several miles away, probably to catch traffic to and from the Hall there. As mentioned Highfield was built later by the NER, perhaps for a basic spot.

In places the NER seemed to enjoy, perversely, labelling the station at first correctly by the nearest village, only to alter things after a time in favour of some place much further off. This was usually to avoid confusion with similar names in other parts of the country, one of the most amusing being Burton Constable near Hornsea, renamed Ellerby, possibly because booking clerks and travellers were likely to confuse it with Constable Burton on the Hawes branch.

On the York - Market Weighton line, in order, Huntington became Earswick, Stockton became Warthill, Gate Helmsley - Holtby, Burnby - Nunburnholme and Shipton - Londesborough. On the Market Weighton - Beverley line of 1864 even Dalton Holme was changed for the name of the nearest habitation, the farm at Kiplingcotes; Cherry Burton kept its splendid nameboards.

The fourth section of line, that from Market Weighton to Driffield opened on 1st May 1890, the result of a watered down plan of 1884 to construct a line from Scarborough to Howden which would be known as the Scarborough, Bridlington & West Riding Railway, to be accepted in a truncated form to Market Weighton. The NER offered to work the nominally independent line between Driffield and Market Weighton. In many ways the idea of the whole run of line was pointless, running as it would have done over similar terrain and missing out Bridlington by cutting across directly from Seamer to Nafferton. In the event the only sticking point for a time was whether the new station at Bainton was to be furnished with a level crossing or a road overbridge.

3. The line is opened

The openings of various parts of the new railway system are given some coverage in local newspapers, with an obvious absence of rejoicing as often found elsewhere. One local report was of the first train which travelled the distance from York to Market Weighton in 1847, on which:-

> 'A numerous and respectable party of gentlemen celebrated this important event by dining at the Devonshire Arms Hotel in the latter place, having had an excursion from York. There was food, champagne, food piled high on the tables and speeches from important people.'

Miss Martin of the Beverley Reference Library very kindly beavered away to find two references in the Beverley Guardian, the first from the issue of 1st May 1865 which carried the following report of the opening of the further stage to Beverley:

Holtby station, looking north. One of the finest on the line and the best of G.T. Andrews' designs. Note milepost No.9 still in position.
Copyright: K. Hoole Collection.

A snapshot of Stamford Bridge from the train. The same design as Holtby. *Copyright: C.T. Goode.*

'On Monday last the line was opened without any ceremonial, the first train leaving Hull for York via Market Weighton at 6.40am., and one in the opposite direction at 7.10am. The trains, on their arrival at stations between Beverley and Market Weighton were received by the wondering inhabitants of the district with admiration, the boys doing their full share in honour of the event by heartily cheering. The holding of an important agricultural show at Market Weighton in July next will doubtless be a most memorable event in this ancient market town. It will then most likely be visited by thousands who have never before been there. All who may do so will be satisfied with the productiveness of the district.

On the occasion of the opening of the above line, Mr Jackson, the Contractor, gave a substantial dinner of roast beef and plum pudding to about 200 of his workmen, which was provided by Mr Simpson of the Londesborough Arms Hotel, Market Weighton, in first class style and and was served up in a large building kindly lent for the occasion by T. W. Rivis Esq., The Rev. Mr. Ebsworth, the highly respected curate, occupied the chair and T. J. Jefferson Esq. the vice-chair. After the usual loyal toasts the health of the contractor T. Jackson Esq. was given by the chairman in an appropriate speech, the company rising and drinking his health in musical honours, with three times three and three cheers for his father; the healths of Mr. Thomas, the agent and Mr Dixon, the manager and other officials under Mr Jackson were given and the navvies gave them cheer after cheer. The chairman then gave the health of the navvies in a kind and most instructive speech, winning the respect of the company by the unassuming manner in which he discharged his duties as chairman.

Stamford Bridge station today. Much the same, except for a single storey section at the front. The trackbed leads to the end of the railway viaduct. Copyright: C.T. Goode.

After the healths of the chairman and vice chairman were given, the company broke up at about half past seven, well pleased with the kind treat.

It should be added that the navvies behaved themselves in a most respectful manner, not even a wrong word being heard amongst them'.

The above report is printed, not merely because it has been found, but because of the charming style and elegance it offers.

The reporter in the Eastern Daily News puts a slightly different slant on the same event and has a sly dig at the locals:

'The only inconvenience arising from the running of the trains appeared to be that which was so sagely foreseen by the opponents of railways in the days of George Stephenson - the disturbing of the peace of mind of the occupants of the meadows and the pilferers of the corn fields. The trains during the day ran with remarkable punctuality, but attracted no extraordinary number of passengers. The passenger traffic between York, Hull and the north must either be very limited, or people cautious of availing themselves of a cheaper and readier route, in such a hurry as it was supposed they would do. It may be that a anxiety exists to see that everything is in working order, and that prudential motives may account for the fewness of travellers yesterday. It is probable, however, that the NER will suffer little by loss of traffic on the Hull and Selby line and that the development of a new traffic on the Hull, Beverley and Market Weighton will fully compensate, as well as give a dividend on the outlay for the new works. It is strange, however, that the Market Weighton people are not sanguine as to improved trade and its concomitant - accumulation of wealth.

As a body they urge that large dealers in commodities - sellers or buyers - will seize the advantages offered by the railway to come to Beverley or Hull and so deprive the people of Market Weighton of some of the little business that has hitherto been carried on there. How little this has been is apparent from a very brief visit. Some, however, say that when such is the case, things unable to get worse, they must mend; so it will probably be with Market Weighton, in spite of the croakers.

Increased railway facilities tend to improve the social condition of a people and the opening of the new line may prove beneficial in this respect. On enquiry as to the mode of conducting the parish business it was shown that its management was in the hands of surveyors of highways, churchwardens and others. Thinking that a town of some 2,000 inhabitants should adopt some more modern system of self-government, one of the most important financial officers of the place was appealed to, when that functionary confessed that he did not know what the 'Local Government Act' meant. His darkness may probably be dispersed when daily newspapers reach the town in larger numbers than they have hitherto done'.

It was noted finally that the Beverley and Market Weighton coach ceased running some six weeks earlier, the proprietor wisely declining to compete with rail and await his fate, that of being 'run off the road'.

The Driffield Times reported the opening of the line to Market Weighton in its issue of Sat. 3rd May 1890:

'This line of railway, over which goods trains have been running for the past weeks, was opened for passenger traffic on Thursday morning. A large company assembled at Driffield to witness the arrival and departure of the first train, and punctually to time at 6.40am. it steamed into the station, when some twenty or thirty people availed themselves of an early ride on the new line. The train was in charge of an inspector'.

4. The Line described. Bootham Jc. to Stamford Bridge.

Our way was shared at first with the line to Scarborough, using in York station one of the bays Nos. 4-7 at the north end. The run passed north by the signal box at Burton Lane, where the Foss Island branch took off eastwards to serve the south end of Rowntree's cocoa works which passed by on the east side of our route for some distance, matched by six neat rows of housing built for that firm's workforce and running along the opposite side. North of this activity was a skew crossing with the main road to Helmsley at Bootham Jc., the signal box (1m. 1259 yd. from York) on the east side, beyond which the double track of the Beverley line departed to the northeast. The crossover here was of interest in that it was placed well south of the road crossing well away from the junction points and with a necessary heavy pull of the lever operating it. The gates here were known as Bootham Stray, while adjacent was a herdsman's cottage, a little further off to the east of the intriguingly named Mille Crux farm.

The once capacious goods shed now appears to be a sports hall with a piece of equipment on display outside. The area is very well kept.
Copyright: C.T. Goode.

ENGLISH ARMY MARCHES NORTH ....

BOTH ARMIES MEET AT STAMFORD BRIDGE.....

Some of the old battle scenes depicted by local school children in the centre of Stamford Bridge. The third strip down and the bottom one shows the river crossing.   *Copyright: C.T. Goode.*

A short run brought the passenger to Earswick station (0.1375yd.) the first of those stops which were renamed here presumably to avoid confusion with Huntingdon. The culprit lies one mile to the north by the river Foss, over which the railway passed before entering the station. Adjacent to this crossing was a roadway over the line to Haxby via Earswick, which left the latter village well and truly on the wrong side of the river for rail passengers. However, restricted access was provided over the water to what appears to have been a neatly laid out place, with all its recreational facilities set out on the west side round the "Folk Hall". The signal box at Earswick lay on the south side to the west of the level crossing with the Strensall road, and beyond were the parallel platforms with the principal building on the north side, a glorified standard single storey platelayer's house of twin end-on gables linked by a central section. There was a standard wooden shelter with a sloping roof for York passengers. Before the crossing and signal box were reached came, first the main crossover, then a short siding on the south side, while behind the station on the north side were two roads serving coal drops and general goods, and a short siding to the Ebor Timber works and Clarence Leather Company. The latter premises were huge for the site chosen, of three storeys and in three bays, plus chimney.

The line now passed over Huntington Lane crossing and beneath the new bridge of the thirties carrying the coastal traffic on the A64. Trains were permitted a line speed of 70mph. or more before reaching Warthill station after a long run of 3m. 1168yd., to a point where the line turned south east for a long, straight stretch to Market Weighton. Gradients were mostly light, the worst being 1 in171 westward to milepost 19 and 1 in 181 westwards again near milepost 8. In 1909 Warthill station was a lonely place on a common with nothing but a rectory for company and with the village of Stockton-on-the-Forest a mile away to the southwest. Warthill village did not really come into the picture, being a right turn north of the station, then a further right at the crossroads and straight on over a different level crossing. The crossing at the west end of the station had the signal box on the north side along with the main station building which was a G. T. Andrews standard design, with the long side end-on and two storeyed with a bay window to the platform, a siding to the road and coal drops, with the main crossover between the two outlets. Things were to change here when the Sand Hutton Light Railway appeared some years later; more is given about this interesting little line later on. The first lifting barriers to be used on a level crossing in this country appeared at Warthill during the fifties - quite why just here is not certain, however the NER at York were known as trend setters and the local engineers had already set up low barriers which rolled horizontally on wheels for the difficult gates at Walton Street, now barriers, though the other set still survives at Melton Lane Crossing near Brough, and at the station.

The next station was Holtby (1m.1632yd.), approached through a moderate cutting and up a gradient of 1 in 250, then beneath a rare commodity, a road bridge. Here too the platforms were parallel to each other and the station building was on the north side, a large one, in fact it might be wondered whether someone had made a mistake here, as the structure was top grade and the equal of Stamford Bridge with the long two storeys end-on to the line, with a recess and four pillared canopy to the platform, though there was no pillared entrance to the road as at Stamford Bridge. Here, though, there was no safe means of crossing the line for passengers other than the porter's barrow way, as the approach road off the bridge was long and there was no similar approach to the York platform. No stations on the Hull & Barnsley had footbridges: passengers had to take pot luck! Holtby signal box was on the south side and required no strain to work the only coal drop siding and main crossover. Clearly some spec. builder must have gone astray here. Gate Helmsley lay half a mile to the south on the A166, while Holtby lay a further two miles thereon to the south west. Perhaps the NER had its eye on the landed properties at Upper Helmsley and Sand Hutton to the north. Today the station building is still there but hardly visible from the bridge due to the encroaching wood.

Along now to Stamford Bridge station (1m.359yd) across the 90ft high viaduct crossing the Derwent. The bridge has 16 brick arches and a central span elegantly made of cast iron. This is still the only large viaduct of its kind in the East Riding. Stamford Bridge station was a neat installation with coal drops and a run-round line to a goods shed behind the station on the north side, where the station building is situated next to the road crossing. The building is similar to Holtby but is a G. T. Andrews' special, that is with a pillared porte cochère facing the road as well as the pillared recess to the platform. The future of the building seems secure as a conversion to flats. On the south side a single siding trailed in to the York direction, while at the end of the parallel York platform was a wind pump. The signal box was east of the level crossing and, for some time earlier controlled an extra crossover to the west of the viaduct for single line working in an emergency, as well as the usual one at the east end of the layout. There was at one time a large house, Derwent Hill to the south of the station, while the village itself was no great distance away to the north. The original Stamford Bridge is shown on maps to have been a few yards upstream from the newer one, and at certain times of the year the area is liable to severe flooding.

Fangfoss is an unusual building for the line, having a central gable and bay to the platform. A caravan site is off to the left, premises being a shop and office.   *Copyright: C.T. Goode.*

5. Fangfoss to Pocklington

From Stamford Bridge the line is more or less level, but straight and runs over common land past gatehouses at High Catton and Full Sutton, where was once a large aerodrome, now a prison to reach Fangfoss (Frangefos or Frank's ditch) (2m.1127yd) where, for the first time platforms were staggered, the northern one being encountered first. The signal box was at the level crossing on the south side, then over it the station building was met at the near end of the other platform, an Andrews usual type of structure forming a little landmark on the curve of a minor road which runs to the crossing at this point. Opposite here to the north was a general goods siding and weighing machine, plus two parallel lines serving the coal drops which trailed into a long siding to form a shunting neck. At some later date than 1909 the long siding became a loop which eliminated a slip across the running lines, this being restored to

Pocklington from the side of West Green signal box, where the signalman takes an interest. A Hull -bound dmu is in the platform.
Copyright: K. Hoole Collection.

West Green signal box and starting signal from a York-bound dmu in the station. Copyright: C.T. Goode.

Pocklington School uses the station as a sports hall, complete with roof and entrance porch. Copyright: *C.T. Goode.*

its normal form even later on. Coal was an important part of every NER station yard, as the station masters were allowed to sell coal to the local populace as a business with a profit for themselves. The hiring of sacks to farmers was also undertaken. Fangfoss lay 1½ m. to the north east with a larger village, Wilberfoss off in the other direction. One would imagine that revenue here would be extremely poor, except during wartime when RAF personnel would use the facilities for leave to and from Full Sutton nearby. Today the station building stands proudly adorned with its working clock and a few restored metal ads. in the middle of a thriving caravan centre.

The line now began to climb slightly past Yapham Gatehouse, where there was a halt in early days, to Pocklington (4m.695yd.), first over the west road into the town, then over the second at West Green, where a signalman was stationed in a small cabin, before the station was reached. The building was one of G. T. Andrews' designs having an all-over roof, very atttractive as such often are with a long, low frontage, a porte cochère in the centre and the station master's house at one end with the all-surveying bay window. Every conceivable office was included; ladies' and gents' facilities, different waiting rooms by class, though not, I believe a bookstall which Driffield and Beverley both had. The boys' school was situated near the west end (hence the signalman perhaps), and would generate much traffic at term-end.

The goods yard was sandwiched between the east end of the station and the level crossing taking traffic to and from the Hull-York road some distance away. The yard was formed of two roads parallel to the running lines with a large goods depot, to similar lines to coal drops and a general goods siding. On the opposite side of the line was a siding to the gas works and a 1¼ mile branch to the flour mill of J. Thirsk. On this side were also cattle sidings adjacent to the main line.

Fortunately the frontage of the station and the covered area have been preserved by the school for use as a sports hall.

A view looking from the main Pocklington signal box looking west through the station just after closure.   *Copyright: C.T. Goode.*

6. Nunburnholme to Market Weighton.

Nunburnholme came next (2m.458yd.) with staggered platform in what I have always deemed the correct mode, in that a train could run in beyond the level crossing into its platform on the both sides, getting clear of the road as here. There was thus no danger of a train, when stopping, running beyond and through the gates; stopping was always the greatest worry of a steam driver. Here the station house, of single storey, was on the north side and signal box on the south, the yard being small, behind the platform on the north side with a general siding to the road, a loading dock and a single slip across the running lines. The main building is, today, a beautifully preserved house. The original choice of station name, Burnby was correct as the village was only a short walk away, while Hayton was close on the opposite side. Any carriage trade would have been encouraged to come from Warter Priory, a little further than 3½ miles to Nunburnholme, which was of negligible size. Nunburnholme station closed early, on the first day of April in 1951.

Nunburnholme was another different station from the usual run, firstly by closing earlier than most and also by have twin gables to the road, here neatly filled in for its role as a private dwelling.

Copyright: C.T. Goode.

Londesborough tries to hide modestly behind a tree in its adopted village of Shiptonthorpe. The track layout here was minimal, with bits fitted into what the road allowed. Copyright: C.T. Goode.

The Wolds are now showing their hand fairly close at hand; the highest spot is 539ft. East of the station a fall of 1 in 171 had at its foot Avenue Lodge, where George Hudson had his personal halt at the end of a long avenue some three miles long which extended to the York-Hull road and flanked by trees in the French fashion. It is assumed that the Avenue was there before the line; parts of it are left but of the original hall only the terrace survives and, of course a vast park which can be walked through either from Towthorpe or Londesborough village. The older hall was later rebuilt.

A short way further and Londesborough was reached (1m.1734yd.) set at the north end of Shiptonthorpe village (itself an amalgam of Shipton and Thorpe-le-Street), which was large enough in 1910 to raise some revenue; the station remained open until the line closed. The site had only minimal facilities with a siding to a loading dock on the down side and siding to

Soon after nationalisation, or around that time, the railway press office under the enthusiastic guidance of George Dow commissioned a photo survey of various parts of the railway. Market Weighton was included, as the following excellent prints show. Here, looking west, the station manages to look neat and tidy, even with its poor canopies. There are plenty of seats, notices and adverts., but the lighting is feeble. Copyright: BR Public Relations, York.

coal drops on the up. The platforms were parallel, with the signal box on the York side of the level crossing. The G. T. Andrews gable and structure with platform bay window stood prominently at a junction of roads, today much as in railway days. This balanced the ancient little church round at the side of the main road. Londesborough Park was a good 2½ miles up a rising road. The station was renamed in 1867, presumably after Hudson's demise.

Market Weighton (to West signal box 1m.1636yd.) managed to make a greater splash on the railway map than did all other places on the line, due to its becoming a junction at its location as a convenient crossing place of four routes; the Romans could certainly recognise a good place when they saw one, many years earlier. All the railway activity went on to the north of the town, and the York-Hull road passed beneath the Selby line at the west end, causing a minmum of inconvenience and going its own way up Arras Hill at the east end. Only the A163 northwards to Bainton passed over a level crossing at the west end of the station platforms. The station had a footbridge here, outside the overall roof which spanned the platforms in the same manner as at Pocklington, with the low, station premises facing due south. The style of these tended to vary at each place: Beverley's and Driffield's were rather fine, presumably because they enjoyed a very prominent position, Filey's reasonable, while at Market Weighton there was little to write home about, a plain affair with five chimney stacks, each larger than the height of the premises they were sitting on, and a small porte cochère of two pillars. Being in need of heavy repairs the roof went, with Driffield's, in 1947, both producing a ghastly form of bracketed awning in their place, and the rest went after closure at Weighton after a lorry collided with the porch in front. Baddeley states in the Yorkshire guide for 1897 that the town presented its worst side to the railway, singling out the gasworks and church for special condemnation - actually the avenue from the station passed straight across open land with the gasworks away to the left, though when he wrote a large cattle market would make the atmosphere fragrant close by when in operation. All Saint's church stood at the far end overlooking the market place and, in my opinion would have nothing to do with the first impressions, being a fine building with, today, a well decorated ornate roof within.

By 1910 the cattle had gone, replaced by a court room and police station and, in the course of time a wooden hut was added at the west end housing the useful and handy Tessa's tearoom.

Here, from the west end, canopies seem more gaunt. The signal box with its laterr concrete steps is in evidence, as is the footbridge, fine bracket of two junction signals for York and Selby and long filling pipe from the water tank. Copyright: BR Public Relations, York.

As far as is clear, the line from York was double throughout, while that from Selby was single though with room to double up if needed. The latter line ran alongside the former for a short way, to join at the road crossing. Some way out of town was a farm controlling a siding to a gravel pit, and during 1850 the Selby line was doubled from Market Weighton to this point. The line out of the station to the east to Beverley was also single at first, probably due to financial problems, with a passing place at Kiplingcotes, later a double to single line there, and a single to double line at Cherry Burton, the alterations happening as traffic and money dictated, however, on the opening of the line to Driffield which was double from the outset in 1850 it was decided to double the rest, this christened by a new service of trains between Hull and Selby via Market Weighton, probably to take the strain off the Brough route. This would not last for any great length of time.

The yard layout here was concerned with filling the available space, the Selby line running in as normal, though the outgoing line came off immediately after the level crossing and running on for a few yards before joining up with its fellow. This was probably the original single line. Opposite was a cattle dock next to West signal box, with a further one on a short line opposite. On the other side of the crossing at the west end of the platform was a water tank and extended filling pipe, essential for replenishment for homebound excursions or those about to tackle the bumpier parts of the line - there was another supply at the east end as well. North of the station was a warehouse and, joined to this the engine shed of two roads, one running through to a turntable. There was also a siding parallel to the running lines. On the south side was a long siding running east and curving round with the Beverley branch for a short way. At first this had no connection, but was later given a slip across the running which also gave the East Jc. a main to main crossover. From this long siding lines were thrown off to the goods shed, and oil depot, two lines for the coal drops and the gasworks, which was probably not rail linked. The East signal box was also on the north side and situated rather out of the hurly-burly, controlling the north junction which was normal and the aforementioned slip line to the yard.(0.453yd.) When the line to Beverley was single, there was a normal crossover sited in the usual place ahead of the junction points.

What is never mentioned was the interesting range of original NER hardware of signal parts, posts, some of them tall, and brackets at this station, typical of the flamboyancy of the period and which would be expensive to provide and, no doubt, just as costly to remove.

The engine shed opened along with the York branch and housed one engine, though little is known about its activities. In

1908 the engine was rostered to work to Driffield, then back through to Selby and return to Market Weighton by mid-afternoon. The shed would offer refuge to yard shunters, would hold pilot engines available to assist at the head of ailing engines on excursion up Endthorpe bank, though latterly these were usually attached at Selby, and turned the engine on the pick-up goods train if the elements were howling from the wrong direction, probably quite unofficially. Often tenders would be low and cabs wide open.

Twenty years later, a recovery train headed by a diesel shunter passes the same spot. The water crane is still there as is Tessa's (presumably closed) tea room. Copyright: C.T. Goode.

7. The Final Run to Beverley.

We are now entering the third and final stretch, the prettiest with speeds now once more allowable up to 70mph. after the slack through the turns of Market Weighton. There were climbs at 1 in160 up to the summit of 184ft. beyond Kiplingcotes and a steady descent almost into Beverley. The road has the worst of it with a climb of fair length up to 430 ft. on Arras hill, but an unsurpassed view right across to Pateley Bridge and down to Lincoln cathedral. The line found its way in the lee of this hill to the north and another running to 438ft. on the other side, soon becoming single originally until 1830 and running south of Godmanham where the NER would have liked a station. Before this a bridge carrying the old Roman road north crossed over; this became the pleasant walk from Towthorpe into Londesborough Park. Originally the land here which was somewhat boggy belonged to the Rev. Blow of Goodmanham and the railway ran by a stream which was partly diverted to form the bed of the line. Upwards past a mill and rifle range north of the line until the line made a perceptible bend towards the south east over what was described as 'the peculiarly constructed bridge', actually a skew brick span over the road with cleverly laid strings of brickwork in its curvature, to reach Dalton Holme station (3m. 493yd.) with the signal box on the south side and no level crossing for a change. The main building was a G. T. Andrews standard design on the north side with all the facilities for what must have surely been a sparse run of passengers. The south side had the usual wooden shelter with pent roof. A small yard was west of the station on the north side, the three short sidings buffers to the station offering weighing machine, loading dock and a line running through a small goods shed. A single slip connection ran into the York direction of running. At first the yard layout had the same sidings coming off the Hull line, facing, before the double line became one at the northerly partform. This was apparently Lord Hotham's station (eventually) and was something of a damp squib, as his country seat was two miles on to the east.

The tea room is prominent here at the side of the forlorn station frontage at Market Weighton. Not much design here, methinks.
Copyright: C.T.Goode.

Lockington, with a superior building, lay almost as far away still further east on the Hull-Bridlington line. The revenue from Kiplingcotes is something of a mystery, as is the date when the name of the place was changed. The NER kept that station in top form and would bring out new and interesting rolling stock to be photographed here, away from the town pollution. On closure, Mrs. Uttley of Tessa's tearoom came to live here and the building received a cover of grey stone wash. Both it and the signal box survive, being first a tea stop, then a furnishing business taking in the goods shed as well.

The Hothams reside in the village of South Dalton and have ancestors going back to William the Conqueror. The first baronet was Sir John, Parliamentary Governor of Hull, then there was Admiral Hotham who became Baron Hotham of South Dalton in 1797, which the incumbent at the time of the opening of the line was the local MP. At this period, in 1861 was erected Dalton Holme church, the spire of which at 200ft. is visible from many parts of the county. In grey stone, the building was designed by J. Pearson, architect of Truro cathedral, and completed for £20,000.

Kiplingcotes station building still looks the part, twenty years after closure.   *Copyright: C.T. Goode.*

The line proceeded eastwards, crossing lands owned at one time by Major Dawson and the Vicar of St. Mary's Beverley, to arrive at Cherry Burton (4m.406yd.), an ancient village of 500 at the time of the line's opening and with one of the prettier names to puzzle over. It lay just south of its station, with Etton equidistant to the north, offering good possibilities from both sides. No level crossing here either, with a smart iron bridge over the B1248 on its long and today busy route to Malton. The bridge over the B1248 has been removed, though the way of the line is open to ramblers, leaving a dangerous spot at which to cross, though the council has done its best with suitable warnings. The station building was on the south side and owed more to the NER pattern found elsewhere and not of the Andrews style at all. It was two storeyed, long and plain, of mellow brick. The signal box was at the far end of the opposite platform, controlling the small yard, the buffer stops of which faced the station approach. There were three sidings for a goods shed, coal drops and cattle dock. On the diagram to hand no main crossover is shown, though one would certainly

Even the waiting shed clings on to life.   Copyright: C.T. Goode.

Cherry Burton station was really an oblong house with the bay window added centrally on the platform.   Copyright: C.T. Goode.

be provided. Pre 1881 the lever frame was on the main York platform and controlled passing of the single line from one side to the other on the formation. After July 1881 a double line arrived from Beverley to fill the formation, becoming single to serve the one platform and continue on to Kiplingcotes. Such changes must have been rather confusing for the staff at times.

Cherry Burton was in early times the seat of Addi, a Saxon earl who may well have lent his name to nearby Etton, since one reference gives 'Cherry' not as from the fruit, but from 'Caedhers', a local Saxon noble. However , in 1201 Lord Percy's wife gave to the Knights of St. John the manor of North, or Cherry Burton, the South being Bishop Burton. Mr. D Burton was the landed gentleman when the line was built, living either at Low Hall Etton, Cherry Burton Hall or High Hall, Bishop Burton. The latter is now the local agricultural college.

A recent view of Cherry Burton from the approach, fitted with bow windows each side of the approach. Copyright: *C.T. Goode.*

Cherry Burton signal box was rarely photographed, like the station. Son Chris plays the part of signalman here, with no levers.

Copyright: C.T. Goode.

The yard at Cherry Burton is now separate from the station building and is used by a haulier, while it is not clear what the old goods shed, smaller than Stamford Bridge's, contains.   Copyright: C.T. Goode.

There remains the final run down to Beverley North Jc. (3m.283yd.), where the line curves smartly to join the Bridlington line. The line passed beneath a minor road or two, then in a chalk cutting some 100 ft. long to pass beneath the main A164 at Molescroft, then over land owned at construction by Mr. W Bainton. Round about here was little of elegance except for Park House on the south of the line. Beverley station lies a short way from the site of the Junction and is fully dealt with in the companion 'Hull & Scarborough Railway'.

The curving east end of Market Weighton, taken at some time in the 1930s. A shot train has left for the Driffield line, while a tank engine waits in the goods line on the right by the other water crane. Notable is the tall home signal to halt westbound trains, while the branch bracket signal for eastbound carries the splitting distants below it, only one of which is renewed, to give a most untidy effect.

Copyright: K. Hoole Collection.

8. The passenger Workings.

From the outset in 1847 there were three trains each way on weekdays on both the York and Selby lines. In 1850 the Selby trains which had stops only at Holme and Dubwith (sic) were reduced to two each way and the York service was shown as follows:

from York: 9.10am.,2.15pm.
from Market Weighton   7.30am.,10.45.,5.30pm.

On Tuesdays a train ran from Market Weighton at 6.30am., calling at all stations and meeting a train at Selby for Hull and Leeds markets. This was later started back from Pocklington. A coach left Beverley for Market Weighton at 9.15am., connecting with the 10.45am., and returning with passengers off the 2.15pm. from York. In these early days the railway company (Y&NM) was careful to work closely with any road transport likely to be on hand.

In 1855 the new NER had:

from York: 9.05am.,2..30pm.,7.00pm.
from Market Weighton: 7.30am.,10.35.,5.35pm.

These stopping trains took 1¼ hr. for the distance. A note added that on York, Pocklington and Market Weighton market days trains would stop at Yapham Gate five minutes after leaving Fangfoss or Pocklington . On the occasion of the York fortnightly fairs the 7.30am. would leave at 6.0am. and be earlier throughout. There was also the now regular Tuesday service from Pocklington to Selby, dep: 6.00am. and arr. at 7.15am. to connect with the services for Leeds and Hull markets. All the Selby line stations were now shown, as well as Holme and Bubwith.

In 1858 the pattern was much the same:

from York: 9.05am.,2.56pm.,7.00.
from Market Weighton: 7.30am.,10.25.,5.30pm.

The 7.30 was still liable to set off at 6.00 on Tues. for the reason mentioned, and needed watching. Yapham Gate was again mentioned as a stop on market days, while a new extra ran on Weds. only from Stamford Bridge to Market Weighton at 12.30pm., arr. 1.40pm. stopping at all stations.

By 1870 the line to Beverley had been open for five years and the third class fare shown for York to Beverley was 2/10- (14p). The timetable entry was compressed with four trains each way:

from York: 6.55am.,9.50., 3.25pm.,7.05
from Beverley: 6.55am.,9.43.,1.35pm.,5.00.

A service left Market Weighton for Hull at 2.30pm. Neither Kiplingcotes nor Cherry Burton had appeared as yet. A little later on the running time for the stopping trains stabilised at two hours. An express from Hull appeared, leaving at 1.15pm. and calling at Beverley, Market Weighton, Pocklington and Stamford Bridge; this connected at York with the 2.55pm. Scotch Express.

1895 now and the timetable began to look much as it was in its final form. All the station names were present and any renaming had been carried out. Apart from the faster trains stopping at the principal stops at Beverley, Market Weighton and Pocklington, the slower ones always stopped at all the stations, none having been singled out as on other lines elsewhere.

from York: 6.40am.,9.00.,11.40.,2.50pm.A., 4.55.,8.05.
from Hull: 6.50am.,9.52.,12.20pm.B., 2.10.,4.27.,7.35.

Trains A and B stopped only at Cottingham, Beverley, Market Weighton, Pocklington and Stamford Bridge, all others by request, the journey taking 1½ hr. In 1885 there had been only five trains each way and the fast workings needed 1¾ hr.

Past the turn of the century to 1910 and Newcastle was shown as an arr/dep. time to or from York trains. There are eight workings each way and two accelerated ones.

from York:
6.35am.,9.05.,9.57.A.,11.43.,2.47pm.,5.00.,7.00.B., 8.05.
from Hull:
6.50am.,8.25.,9.53.,12.05pm.,1.55.,4.00.,5.05. D., 7.35.

A connects with the 8am. ex Newcastle and stops at Pocklington and Market Weighton only. B connects with the 5.04 ex Newcastle. Makes three stops. C makes three stops plus Stamford Bridge. D took 61 min. and stopped at Market Weighton and Pocklington. Connected with the train for Newcastle arr. 8.03pm.

In the shadow of the Great War in 1914 the following services were to be found, much the same as above:

from York:
6.35am.,9.00.,9.57.,11.45.,2.47pm.,5.00.,7.00.,8.05.
from Hull:
6.50am.,8.20.,9.53.,12.05pm.,4.00.,5.05.,7.35.

Cherry Burton was now marked as 'for South Dalton' and a two minute stop for water or dash to the tea room was allowed at Market Weighton. As the war dragged on services were reduced to five each way; one new feature was a commuter train at 7.30am. from Pocklington to York, arr. at 8.08am. War workers might have been catered for perhaps. In 1918 seven trains were running again, though only five from Hull.

In 1924 with Grouping and the appearance of the LNER, things were becoming more interesting and ambitious. There were seven services each way, with the 8.25am. from Hull taking an hour, with three stops. The 10.05am. from York performed likewise, both with a minute wait at Market Weighton. The development of importance, however was the new Hull to Newcastle restaurant car service which left at 4.47pm. with a conditional stop at Beverley, the stop at Market Weighton, one at Pocklington and a reverse at York to reach Newcastle at 8.19pm. In the other direction the service left Newcastle at 12.10pm. and York at 2.18, reaching Hull at 3.17 with one stop at Beverley only. There would have been time to service the stock for return at 4.47pm. though not perhaps with the same engine. By any standards this was a remarkable achievement, and only the reversal in York would have grated somewhat, though it would have been eay to change the engine, simply dropping the new one on to the rear.

1925 was similar, and departures were as follows:

from York:
7.40am.,9.35SO.,10.05.,12.25pm.,2.18.,2.47.,5.08.,
7.00A.,7.10.,9.35SO.
from Hull: 7.34am.,8.25B.,11.43.,12.42pmC.,4.00.,4.4.,7.32.

The Saturday workings were really trials of a rather curious looking petrol railcar wth a bogie at one end only This worked back from Pocklington at 10.20am., while the evening run was revenue earning one way only, as the car returned empty. The services A and B had three stops only; C stopped only at Beverley.

In 1933 the following train services were available:

from York
7.55am.,10.05A.,12.32pm.,1.55C.,2.42.,5.10.,7.00A.,8.25.
from Hull: 7.15am.,8.25A.,11.45.,4.00pm.,5.00B.,7.37.

A had three stops. B had three stops, took 57 min., then ran through to Newcastle. C stopped at Beverley only, taking 51 min. This ran through from Newcastle.

In 1937 a Sunday train had appeared from York to Bridlington, stopping at Earswick, Stamford Bridge, Pocklington and Market Weighton, to reach the coast at 10.45am. The return working of what was obviously a day excursion left at 8.22pm. with the same stops, reaching York at 9.40pm.

fromYork:7.55am.,10.05.,12.32pm.,2.35C.,2.50.,4.48B.,5.10.
7.00A.,9.24A*
from Hull:
7.15am.,8.25A.,11.25.,12.20pmC.,3.25D.,4.00.,5.00A.,7.30.

An additional service started from Market Weighton at 1.15pm. for York.

Trains marked A made three stops only. B was a non-stop railcar, probably 'Lady Hamilton' which reached Hull at 5.40pm. The C trains were those which stopped at Beverley only but which were not now advertised as through services to or from Newcastle. A* stopped additionally at Stamford Bridge on Saturdays.

This was probably as sophisticated as the timetable was likely to become. A new war was imminent, in spite of 'peace in our time'; the timetable for the end of 1939 was still reasonable however, in spite of a general air of frugality elsewhere.

from York:
7.55am.,10.10A.,12.20pm.,2.55A.,4.48B.,5.10.,6.55.
from Hull:
7.10am.,8.15.,12.30pm.A*.,3.25C.,4.00.,5.00A.,7.20.

A train stopped only three times, except for the 12.30pm. which also called at Stamford Bridge. B ran non-stop to Hull, arr. 5.43. C ran non-stop to York, arr.4.28, with a connection for Newcastle arr. 6.50pm. It must have been quite an unusual experience to run through not just one, but three overall roofs at speed without stopping!

Once the timetables had settled down in 1940, the offerings were as follows:

from York: 7.55am.,10.15A.,12.30pm.,3.10A.,5.10.,7.55.
from Hull: 7.12am.,8.25A.,1.15pm.A.,4.00A.,4.45.,7.17.

The As called at the three main stations, the fastest taking 57 min. (The 4pm.)

When the war ceased in 1945 we were back again to eight trains each way, including a mid-morning 10.25 all-stations train from Hull which took almost 1½ hours. With Nationalisation the timetable included other services via Selby which could also take up to 1½. hours. In 1948 there were eight trains each way via Market Weighton and six shown via Selby.

from York:
7.55am.,10.10.,12.15pm.,3.10B.,5.05.,5.20.,7.15.,9.45.
from Hull:
7.00am.,8.00.,10.30.,12.15pm.,3.10.,4.00.,4.55B.,7.33.
(via Market Weighton)

Four trains from York were semi-fast, as were three from Hull. The B trains had a buffet car and took 1hr. 3min. and 1hr. 9min. A service left Hull for Market Weighton at 8.25am., arriving at 8.58, returning at 9.15, arr. Hull at 9.51. This ran through both Cherry Burton and Kiplingcotes.

Readers will have noticed the absence of Sunday trains in general throughout this survey, apart from the odd Sunday excursion mentioned in 1937. This honoured a request by Lord Hotham that no trains would cross his estate on that day.

Railwaymen could always be divided into those who did not mind the overtime money for the work on the Sabbath, against those who objected, like his Lordship, to turning out on a day of rest and contemplation. It is more than likely that other trains would have been seen on Sunday, especially during the war period. In the official timetable of trains for 1948, the Selby trains are included along with the Market Weighton ones, those on Sundays via Selby being six from York and five from Hull, taking up to two hours in some instances.

In June 1950 a large, easy to read North Eastern Region timetable was produced offering what seemed to be a rich haul of trains, sixteen, until it is broken down into three for the East Coast resorts and five via Selby, the latter taking two hours in some cases as the traveller would have to change once.

fromYork via Beverley:
7.50am.,10.10.,12.15pm.,3.15B.,5.13.,5.30.,7.25.,10,05.

from Hull via Beverley:
7.00am.,7.55.,9.40.12.15B.pm.,3.00SXB,3.57,5.15B,7.33.

B trains were again with buffet cars, plus an extra one SX, covering the run in 61 min. For revellers there was a 10.15SO all stations to Market Weighton.

Quite a strong finish for the steam age then, the knell for which had sounded in 1957, when the diesel units had arrived. As noted, some stations were closed and the overall running time was still roughly one hour. A ghost of earlier times appeared with the return of a summer Saturday 10.27am. Hull-Glasgow restaurant car service which called at Beverley only before York. In 1963 it was altered to 11.10am. and cut back to Edinburgh, being withdrawn in 1964.

In 1960 there was a service of nine trains each way, including the 7.46am. from York and 8.25am. express from Hull, both dmus. The 7.46 enabled Pocklington folk to arrive in Hull for the first time for the start of work at 8.51am.

Twenty five years later and B1. 4.6.0. No. 61276 heads for the hills with a holiday working to the coast. To the left is the open ended portion of the goods shed. The tall signal has a new arm, but the untidy bracket is still the same. Notice the neat topiary and footpath to the East signal box behind the camera.   *Copyright: K. Hoole Collection.*

9. The Motive Power.

Motive power for the York to Hull line reflected the development and change in the types of locomotive available for duties, as with the other routes covered to date, with the exception that York did at times spice up the cake by sending along unlikely locomotives which would perhaps be freshly out-shopped or faced with an otherwise lengthy wait at York shed before a return after an early arrival. Once again the secondary line entertained engines which were past their prime and downgraded to more leisurely duties. These would emanate from York, Botanic Gardens and Dairycoates in Hull. Initially Fletcher's Class 501 2-4-0s would haul the faster trains, with older 675 Class, built in the 1870s with outside frames managing the stoppers. These would find the banks between Beverley and Market Weighton hard work with six or seven four wheelers and all were scrapped by 1890. Old NER -4-4-0s served out their time until 1920 after leaving main line work, after which matters brightened up immensely when Wilson Worsdell's

D49 No.62747 waits at Market Weighton on a Hull-York train.
Copyright: J.W. Armstrong Trust.

R Class came along, the successful D20s to add a little speed and style to some of the heavier trains up to 1939. Even in the 1950s a D20 could be seen on the 7.13pm. from York; one could also be seen on the teatime express from Hull to Bridlington up to around 1958.

The influence of Sir Nigel Gresley's Class D49 4-4-0 locomotives was great, specially designed for secondary passenger work in 1927, but known by the crews as rough riders. Members of this class took over most of the turns until 1957. Up to 1939 members of Class C7 4-4-2s were to be seen on some workings, though they were known to perform badly on any sort of gradient; in spite of this fact, however, they were pressed into use on goods trains over the line from Hull during World War Two and to be seen in some highly unusual locations such as on ballast trains on the Hull and Barnsley. With Dairycoates full of unwilling and expiring C7s and even more unwilling drivers, Botanic Gardens had a total of 15 D49s at one time. Before this the D49s had been the mainstay of running the Hull-Newcastle expresses over relatively flat terrain.

B1 No.61074 negotiates the curves at Market Weighton with a coastwards express   *Copyright: J.W. Armstrong Trust.*

*From rhe footbridge the cattle track siding is seen on the left as B16
No.61438 rounds the curve with a holiday excursion.*

Copyright: J.W. Armstrong Trust.

In the 1950s York would send out the bigger B16 4-6-0s, as
did Hull Dairycoates once it was decided to concentrate a large
number of these engines there. These varied greatly in quality,
the worst of them, more often than not found on day excursions
being more wheeze than action. In 1963 the 8.14am. was a York
B16 turn, shortly before the whole complement was sent off to
Hull, mainly for scrap. However, one last fling was the summer
Saturday working by a Dairycoates B16 on the 11.10am. Hull-
Edinburgh, returning on the 3.20pm. goods from York. Over the
Christmas period B16s appeared on special parcel workings in
the Hull and York areas to supplement the dmus. The 10.05am.
from York was a Doncaster turn and, of NER stock fitted with air
and not vacuum brakes. If no suitable NER engine were
available, an unwitting loco. was purloined off the shed if so fitted,
so that a convenient ex GER B12 4-6-0 would be used; at Hull it
would be given the Banbury Fish to run back to Doncaster.

B1 61068 has the other distant signal 'off' with a stopping train to Beverley. Notice the Station Master's house and a neat flowerbed.

Copyright: J.W. Armstrong Trust.

The 3.40pm. summer Saturday York-Hull often brought in 'foreign' engines from Colwick, Lincoln or Sheffield, more than likely a B1 4-6-0, some of which had obviously never seen a shed cleaner for years. In the late 50s an LM Region engine, perhaps a Black 5 would work the 8.14am. from York; these locos. would presumably be waiting time for return workings on York shed.

Of course the main hot spot was Market Weighton, through which many special workings would come on summer Saturdays via Selby and Driffield, outwards in the late morning and home after tea. Along with the B1s and B16s would come the large and noisier V2 2-6-2s, K1s, K3s and 'Jubilees' from Saltley, Manchester, Liverpool, Holbeck and Farnley Jc. Filey Holiday Camp saw many of them, including 'namers' such as 'E.C. Trench.' (Manchester), "Patriot' and 'Royal Scot' (Farnley) which found itself parked back in a siding at Driffield, due to overcrowding at Bridlington on one occasion in the early 1960s. Even the really big players would appear on such as the Filey-Newcastle trains - north country folk loved Butlin's - though these workings were usually routed by way of Malton (reverse) and Pilmoor Jc. To the author's mind, however, the most praiseworthy were the crews of the little J11 0-6-0s from Barnsley or Rotherham, or the LM 4Fs from Hasland or similar who would forego their goods workings for a time to bring their crowds of anticipating holidaymakers sometimes with difficulty across the Wolds. A pilot engine (D20) was provided at Selby if needed, though the most interesting services provided two engines at source, so that double headed J11s would make a fine and fussy sight.

A K3 from Hull Dairycoates worked the summer weekday 7.3pm,. Filey-York up to 1962.

With the advent of diesel power dmus appeared from the new homes at Botanic Gardens and Leeds Neville Hill, Cravens two car sets from the first and Birmingham C & W four car sets from the latter, with foreign appearances from elsewhere - Derby 3 car sets and Metro-Cammell units. The latter were certainly the best for appearance, good seating and riding quality. From 1960 diesel locos. began to make an impact on services, with English Electric Class 40s on the 5.16pm. Hull-York express and 7.38 return in due course. In summer 1960 a Sulzer Type 2 D5096 was a regular performer on the 8.14am. from York. Often a pair ran in tandem on trains to the coast and the din must have been tremendous! E.E. Type 3, Class 37 went to Dairycoates for freight work, but could be seen on passenger workings such as the 7.38pm. ex Hull. Later, in 1964 the Brush Class 47s were to be found at the head of the 5.40pm. from York.

B16 No.61444 makes a fine sight on the run in to Market Weighton with a heavy return working to the West Riding. Visible is the East signal box - the taller junction signal makes the Beverley route more important. Copyright: J.W. Armstrong Trust.

Quite a lot of the above loco. material has come from a most interesting book by Mr. Stephen Chapman: 'Hudson's Way' produced in York and offering another view of the railway. Apparently Pocklington was the division between Hull and York operating and engineering districts to which, for instance, inspection salons would run before turning round. Both districts kept rather odd vintage engines for this purpose, rebuilt 2-2-4Ts with Nos. 1679 and 190 (York) and Hull's 957 of Class X2 and X3 respectively. After their withdrawal it was a case of using what happened to be nearest the door. At first through freights were in the hands of 0-6-0s, though as these became heavier the B16s 4-6-0s and Q5 0-8-0s took over, with the big wartime step of introducing the thoroughly reliable and hardly ever cleaned 'Austerity' WD 2-8-0s. To be fair, however, one of the class was serviced and out-shopped in shiny black livery - a sight which turned quite a few heads by its rarity.

This may be compared with the cover photograph taken at Kiplingcotes during the early days of the dmus in 1958 when they were in original Clan green livery. The station building still shows its brickwork.

A rather unusual class of engine in an unusual location. BR Standard 4-6-0 No.73167 gets away from Warthill with a local train for York.
Copyright: K. Hoole Collection.

Local pick-up services were run by J27s from York and J25s from Hull, with the stock of seven Ivatt Class 4 2-6-0s and downgraded B1s taking over in time. I assume that the pick-ups ran out from each end to Market Weighton, then returning but transferring the forward wagons at that station. 'Wildebeeste' spent some of her last years on the Bridlington pick-up. The Ivatts had a protective screen on the front of the tender which kept off inclement weather when running in reverse. The older NER varieties did not, and, as noted earlier, hastened to use the 50ft. turntable at Market Weighton if required. The last passenger train from Hull to York was headed by B1 4-6-0 No. 61306, while Class K1 2-6-0 No. 62005 worked the last York-Market Weighton pick-up, then the last literal pick-up on the rail recovery train. Both are now happily employed on preserved railways, along with a J27 No. 65894. For a short time pick-ups were worked by the unusual Clayton diesels, the ones with the high centre cabs. These were unreliable and likely to catch fire, as one did with a returning job at Beverley in the 1960s, holding up the author in a following Cravens dmu. for a good two hours or so until help arrived to shift it.

This photo is a mystery. It shows D49 No.62763 'The Fitzwilliam' and was passed to me as 'leaving Earswick', which it is not, as the background bracket signal would indicate a junction. This would leave Bootham Jc, though the cabin would be on the wrong side of the line. Market Weighton East would be better, though the signals are wrong. Any offers please? Copyright: C. Ord Collection.

Class X2 2-2-4T pressed into passenger service near Cottingham.
Copyright: C.T. Goode.

'Clan Line' at Cattal on one of the circular steam tours of the 1980s.
Super-Steam! (see P. 69) *(see P. 69)* *Copyright: J.C. Clark.*

10. Beeching and All That.

I suppose that it was surprising that the York-Hull line managed to prosper in a modest way for just over a century, and it was perhaps that it did so because it ran directly from the centre of NER influence and management. The patronage of any one of its shareholders or directors living along its path would have helped, but this does not seem to have been the case. Hudson was a damp squib and Lord Hotham tended to exert his influence in the other direction. Several of the stations were, in fact, more decoration than revenue earners; Holtby closed to passengers on 11th September 1939 and to goods on 1st April 1951. Nunburnholme completely on the same day as latterly, Warthill, Fangfoss and Cherry Burton to passengers on 5th January 1959, but Kiplingcotes, due to the original agreement with Lord Hotham, survived as an unstaffed halt. Thus pared down somewhat, and with the new diesel units, BR Eastern Region now considered a modernisation scheme which could easily be maintained by visits from engineers at York. Earlier, too, there had been upgrading with lifting barriers, first in the country, at Warthill in 1953, and colour lights at Market Weighton and near Stamford Bridge. Steel sleepers were laid between Market Weighton and Kiplingcotes.

In 1960 it was decided to try a Central Traffic Control (CTC) scheme, where level crossings would be modernised, large portions of route singled and control maintained from Bootham Jc. at the York end. This would ensure some £7,000 profit each year. In this case the whole line would be single, with two long loops at Pocklington and Market Weighton, where the two signal boxes would remain. Six of the busiest gate boxes would be manned. The junctions at each end would be double becoming single after a short run as is normal practice. Ground frames would attend to what goods yards survived, main signal boxes rebuilt and colour light signalling installed throughout. The total estimated cost would be £83,000, with the York engineer spending £61,000 of this and Hull, which had the shorter section, the rest. Materials were deposited ready for use at Pocklington.

BRITISH RAILWAYS

WITHDRAWAL OF PASSENGER TRAIN SERVICES

WARTHILL, FANGFOSS AND CHERRY BURTON STATIONS

As from 5th January, 1959, the passenger train service will be withdrawn from the undermentioned stations:—

Warthill   Fangfoss   Cherry Burton

ALTERNATIVE FACILITIES FOR PASSENGERS

Warthill

Alternative facilities for Warthill passengers are provided by the East Yorkshire Motor Services Ltd., the West Yorkshire Road Car Company Ltd., and Messrs. Bailey's 'bus services.

Fangfoss

Alternative facilities are provided by the East Yorkshire Motor Services Ltd., and Messrs. Bailey's 'bus services.

Cherry Burton

Alternative facilities are provided by the East Yorkshire Motor Services Ltd.

PARCELS AND OTHER MERCHANDISE BY PASSENGER TRAIN
(Including Passengers' Unaccompanied Luggage)

The existing parcels, etc., collection and delivery service will be continued by British Railways road motor vehicles operating from York and Beverley.

Parcels, etc., addressed "To be called for" or not requiring collection should be addressed to, or handed in at, the stations concerned as at present.

GOODS TRAIN TRAFFIC

There will be no alteration to existing arrangements for dealing with Goods train traffic at these three stations.

The District Traffic Superintendent, British Railways, George Street, Hull (Telephone Hull Central 31739) or the District Traffic Superintendent, British Railways, York (Telephone 53022 Extension 753), or any Station Master in the area, will supply further information or, if desired, arrange for a Railway Commercial Representative to call.

Published by British Railways   (North Eastern Region)   12/58   Printed in Great Britain   R19369 Herald, York   B11

With everything ready to install, the Beeching Report made its nefarious appearance in 1962, carrying a long list of unremunerative lines for closure, among which was the York-Hull line which was described as mainly rural in regard to its passenger services, but with commuter traffic at each end. Each train that ran carried an average of 57 passengers. So far, so good, perhaps, with the operating profit at £5,600. Troubles apparently lay in the cost of track and signalling, which would result in a saving of £43,000 if closure took place. Much was made of the fact that a great deal of revenue came from between Beverley and Hull, as well as from through passengers both elements which would be catered for by existing services. It would seem that the CTC scheme had not been taken sufficiently into account, if at all, to set against the track and signalling deficit, nor had, as in many places elsewhere, the potential for the development of such a line with sensible economies. Some of this sort of action has taken place on both the York-Knaresborough and Bridlington-Scarborough lines.

What was left soon closed quickly; Kiplingcotes and Cherry Burton goods facilities on 27th Janury 1964, Londesborough on 4th May 1965, and Earswick, Stamford Bridge and Fangfoss on 7th June 1965. There was still plenty of freight traffic at Pocklington, which led to the NE Region raising schemes for retaining signal lines between Beverley and Pocklington, and/or Selby, Market Weighton and Pocklingon, as well as more drastic single-line working throughout. Public outcry was furious; the Government changed in 1964, bringing in Barbara Castle, who promised to defer the Beeching plan of closures. This having been said, the Selby-Driffield line was set for closure on 4th June 1965 and the York-Hull for later in the same year, this actually seeing the last train on Saturday, 27th November 1965, a day of heavy snowfall. The 2142 from York was a six car dmu. set packed with many interested parties and enthusiasts.

In retrospect, failures were to implement the CTC scheme sooner, to cut station staff, possibly altogether and to introduce the paytrain system, though the technology was not really available. A little more intelligent marketing would not have gone amiss, especially as, even today, travel by bus is not easy and through passengers via Selby can often take longer than the advertised hour between Hull and York.

Today, if one wishes to catch something of the atmosphere of the old railway and is pressed for time, the best place to look for any structures surviving from the line is Stamford Bridge, where the station building is very much in use and still appears to govern its platforms and beckon in its passengers. Nearby is the railway viaduct, a listed monument which the Selby council, responsible for the west half, wanted to demolish, while the North Wolds council on the eastern side wished to retain. In 1980 the viaduct was sold by BR to the new East Yorks. Borough council for £1 and was duly repaired, one hopes, with the assistance from the Manpower Services Commission. Of Pocklington's preservation we have already heard. Londesborough station building, in Shiptonthorpe, is worth a call. Fangfoss is a happy sort of place, possibly because it is still dealing with public at large, as a shop in the grounds of a caravan park. Much of the railway atmosphere is still there. The site is available off the A1079 through Wilberfoss. Kiplingcotes still has as much as can remain, apart from the track, with a building which now serves teas and furniture, goods shed, signal box and platforms. Access is not easy until one finds a long and narrow lane at the top of Arras hill near the farm which has it name marked on the side of the A1079.

KIPLINGCOTES CLASSIC FURNITURE

(Formerly "Grannies Attic") Established 1959

'Friendly Service' • 'Excellent Value' 'Superb Quality' '100% Family Run' ....'Call In and See Us'....

"Looking for the best value, look no further"

KIPLINGCOTES STATION, MARKET-WEIGHTON, TELEPHONE: (01430) 810284 74 MIDDLE STREET SOUTH, DRIFFIELD www.kcfurniture.co.uk

11. Patronage and Platforms.

In my book, the York, Knaresborough & Harrogate Railway I mentioned that Cattal station was particularly provided with facilities in what seemed to be a poorly populated area. Since then I have received a letter from Mr. J.C Clark of Great Ouseburn who explains this and clarifies still further why other locations are often apparently well endowed.

He mentions that Cattal is now more popular than at any time in its history. He often uses the station from his own village which is some way north across the A59. The point of the letter is that, in earlier years Kirby Hall was situated near the Ouseburns. This was a Georgian manor which was the seat of the Meysey-Thompson family. Between 1850 and 1870 Sir Harry Stephan Thompson was Chairman of the NER, followed by his son Sir Henry (Baron Knaresborough) who held the position until 1923, They are both believed to have used the station regularly and records exist of their being collected by coach from there.

The connection is interesting. It is a pity that the reference missed the book.

12. The Sand Hutton Light Railway.

The line forms an unusual adjunct to the one from York to Beverley, owing its existence to the enthusiasm of Robert James Milo Walker, Third Baronet of Sand Hutton Hall, born on 18th May 1890. He succeeded to the title at the age of ten, after which he obtained a degree at Trinity College, Cambridge and became a major in the Coldstream Guards. It was said of him later that any member of that body needing work was never refused by him. As well as running the estate he also saw to the operation of the village fire service when required, and had a lucrative coal buiness which would immediately put him on a par with local station masters. Above all, however, he was interested in railways and kept in touch with developments in the model railway field through the writings of Henry Greenly and Mr. Bassett-Lowke. He was also a member of the Institute of Transport. In his teens he had operated a large model layout, more than likely '0' gauge, fixed to the railings surrounding the hall grounds using a swing bridge to cross the drive. This, however, did not completely 'fire' him and in 1912 he had ideas for a 15" gauge line to run at ground level in the estate grounds. By the end of 1913 the line was 1,245yd. long and extended to the cricket field in 1914. For its operation a new Bassett-Lowke Class 30 4-4-2 tender engine, 'Synolda' was bought, named after his wife. Needless to say the line was very popular, with postcards available for sale and a Utopian atmosphere of rides, garden parties, cricket, more rides and special rides after Sunday school.

On his return to Sand Hutton after training service in New Zealand during the Great War, Sir Robert and Mr George Batty, his long serving Estate engineer set about an ambitious scheme to extend the railway beyond the estate boundaries to serve the local area; the original proposal was a route from Warthill station to Scrayingham on the other side of the Derwent via Sand Hutton and Bossall, with branches to Claxton and Barnby House, a total of 7½ miles. An Order was confirmed by the

Ministry of Transport in 1920. In May work commenced, using the 15" gauge from Warthill to Sand Hutton and along part of the Claxby branch. It was fast dawning, however, that to cope with the heavier gradients likely to be involved to the east, something meatier than the 15"gauge 'Synolda' was required. By chance almost the whole of the Government's Deptford Meat Depot 12" gauge line was up for sale, solving all problems at one go. Conversion began in 1921 with what was already down suitably widened. 'Synolda' was sold in 1922 and the model era thus came to an end. After many travels and trials 'Synolda' found herself in the Ravenglass & Eskdale Railway museum, according to the last sighting.

Sand Hutton Railway. No.12 taken at the depot in 1927.
Copyright: Rail Archive Stephenson.

First of all the line was completed for goods traffic between Warthill and Claxton, some 4½ miles in 1922, followed by the main line in 1923 which was completed to Bossall by the end of the year, in spite of higher labour costs. The section of line to Scrayingham, birthplace of George Hudson, was abandoned as it would have needed a 100ft. span across the Derwent, provision of which would not have justified costs and labour. Costs per mile throughout were £4,400. The way was single with run-round loops at the termini. Passing places were unnecessary as normally there was only one engine in steam at any time. This also obviated the need for signals. Gradients were stiff east of Sand Hutton with a ruling 1 in 80 for both directions. Warthill station was a gravel path and nameboard next to the station master's garden, while there were three sidings, one running up on to a long brick loading ramp, the centre a line at ground level and the other to the terminus beyond. Between the first two sidings was an NER siding. In 1927 mechanical loading gear was provided to transfer trays of bricks brought from Claxton brickworks. At the Bossall end the halt, with waiting shed, was next to the Buttercrambe road in a pretty, wooded area.

The Track Layout at Sand Hutton

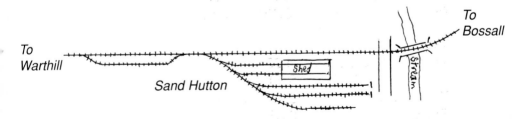

The Deptford locos. were all 0-4-0 well tanks, that is, with the water tank beneath the boiler instead of at each side, built by the Hunslet Engine Co. of Leeds, twelve in all with Nos. 1196-8 built in 1915, 1207 in 1916 and 1288-91 in 1917, to a specification used since 1898. The wheelbase was 3ft.6in., and weight in working order 5 tons 19cwt. Walker purchased four of these, Nos. 1289-91 and 1207, the first called 'Esme' after his second wife, the others numbered 2-4. The engines worked faultlessly, except for a raging thirst for water, needing frequent top-ups. Their cost is not recorded but they must have been a bargain, being almost new. On closure they were soon scrapped in 1932 - practical days indeed. Rolling stock was a set of 75 solidly built four wheeled frames with removable drop-side bodies, each rated 2½ tons or 750 bricks. Hudson's of Leeds supplied a heavy brake van in 1923, some 15ft. long which doubled up on the passenger trains along with another vehicle supplied by them, a fine 6 ton bogie vehicle, 32ft. 9ins. long comprising two compartments with seats for 30 passengers and an extra saloon compartment with six moveable seats for the occupants. This was used as a buffet car during the summer months.

Sir Robert died in 1930, no great age, and the end of the line came soon after with a final year's profit of a mere £1.

There were eight intermediate halts on the main route, and services were almost all on Saturdays only.

1924
Bossall dep:	8.05amx.	12.20pm*.	4.30*
Warthill arr:	8.45	1.00	5.10
Warthill dep:	1.05*	3.05*	5.18*
Bossall arr:	1.45	3.45	5.55

1925
Bossall dep:	12.20pm.	4.30	
Warthill arr:	12.55	5.10	
Warthill dep:	1.05pm.	3.15	5.25
Bossall arr:	1.40	3.55	6.05

1927

Bossall dep:	9.55am.	12.20pm.	4.30
Warthill arr:	10.35	1.00	5.10
Warthill dep:	1.05pm.	3.15	5.25
Bossall arr:	1.45	3.55	6.05

1929

Bossall dep:	12.15pm.	4.30	
Warthill arr:	12.55	5.10	
Warthill dep:	1.05pm.	3.15	5.25
Bossall arr:	1.45	3.45	5.55

* Tea and refreshments served.

X Also Weds only at certain times.

Below are the variants in the spelling of 'Weighton' over the years. There may, of course be others, but these are sufficient to be going on with. It is on record that Little Weighton, not far away, had its original 'Weeton' changed to match, as it were, at some time in its history.

Wegtun	Wichtona	Wihton
Vetun	Whytton	Wichton
Wicotun	Whytthon	Wicton
Wictun	Wycton	Whigheton
Wicstun	Wyhton	Wighton

Wyghton   (the latest of 1472)

Layout plans and gradients

The Main Line

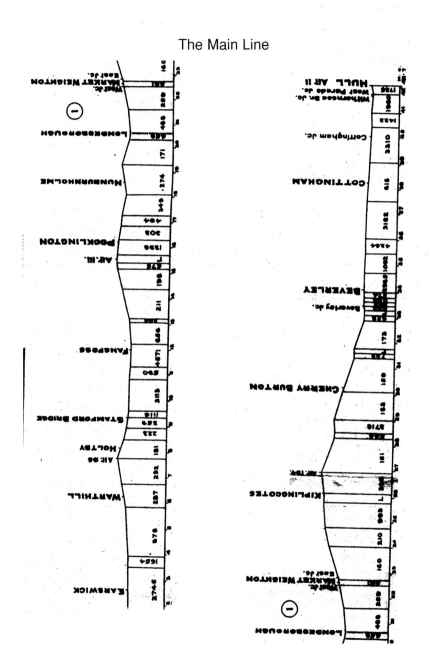

75

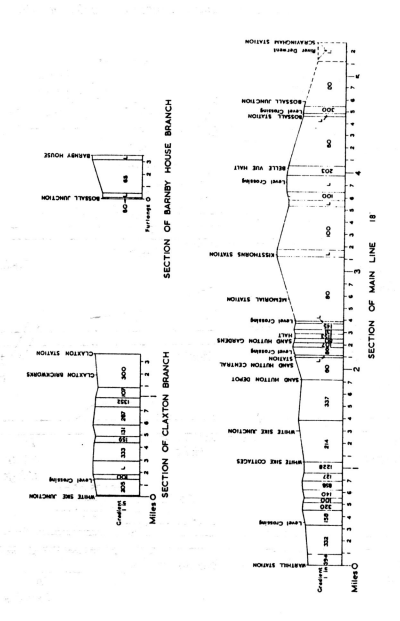

The Sand Hutton Branch

Almost all the following plans are based on the O/S of 1910.

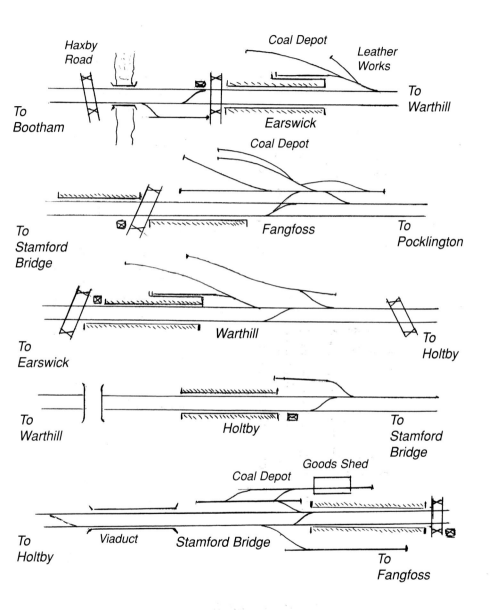

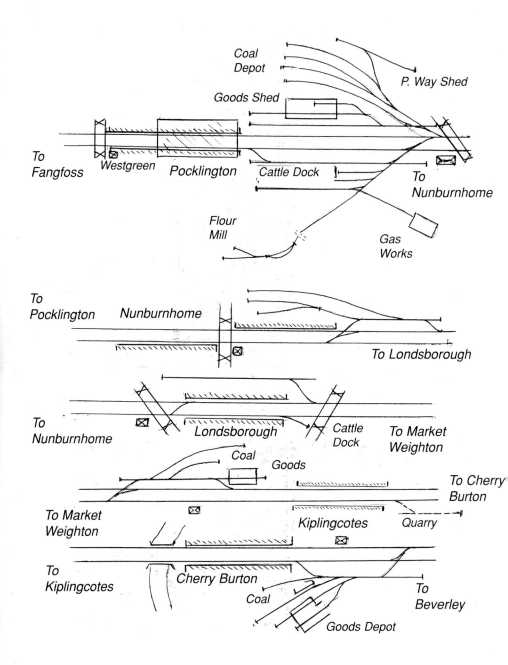

Coal
Depot

P. Way Shed

Goods Shed

To
Fangfoss Westgreen Pocklington Cattle Dock

To
Nunburnhome

Flour
Mill

Gas
Works

To
Pocklington Nunburnhome

To Londsborough

To
Nunburnhome Londsborough Cattle
Dock

To Market
Weighton

Coal Goods

To Cherry
Burton

To Market
Weighton Kiplingcotes Quarry

To
Kiplingcotes Cherry Burton

Coal

To
Beverley

Goods Depot

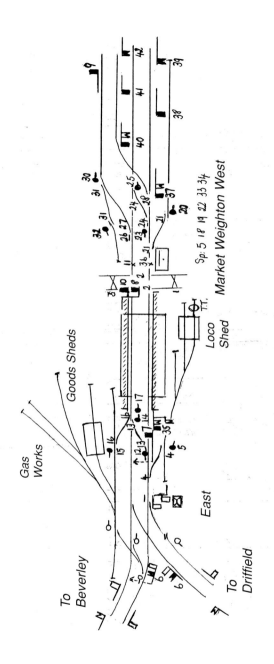

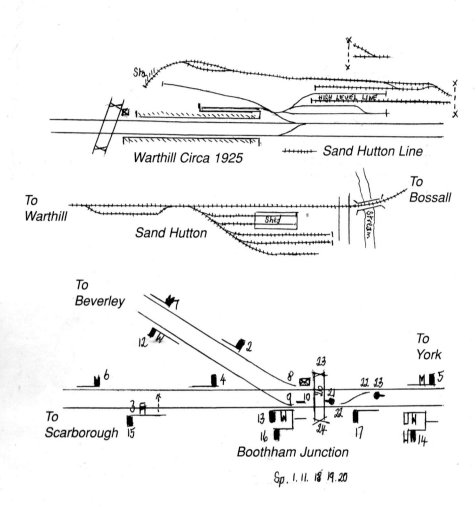

Warthill Circa 1925 ┼┼┼┼┼ Sand Hutton Line

To Warthill

Sand Hutton

To Bossall

To Beverley

To York

To Scarborough

Boothham Junction

Sp. 1. 11. 18 19. 20